How Many Hands to Home

How Many Hands to Home

Lisken Van Pelt Dus

Mayapple Press 2025

Copyright © 2025 by Lisken Van Pelt Dus

Published by   Mayapple Press
                     362 Chestnut Hill Road
                     Woodstock, NY 12498
                     mayapplepress.com

ISBN 978-1-952781-23-0
Library of Congress Control Number: 2024948135

Acknowledgements:

With thanks to the editors of these journals and anthologies in which the following poems first appeared, sometimes in different versions and/or with different titles: *Beltway Poetry Quarterly*: "After the Dying"; *Centrifugal Eye*: "Four Postcards"; *The Bond Street Review*: "Ghazal: Home"; *The Comstock Review*: "Between Damage and Lighthouse" (Special Merit Award, Muriel Craft Bailey Contest), "Lemon Tree," "In the Beginning," "Oh, My Beloveds," "The Wandering Albatross"; *Eunoia Review*: "On the Origin of Love"; *Möbius, The Poetry Magazine*: "How to Become a Raft," "Marta," "Sew Me into Your Country"; *Movable Type*: "Edmonia Lewis Carves Hagar"; *Naugatuck River Review*: "One of Those Towns Lined with Empty Factories" (Finalist, Winter/Spring 2024 contest); *Pirene's Fountain*: "Ode to the Universe" (Pushcart Prize nomination); *Sky Island Journal*: "And If It Is Beautiful," "The Fire Responds to Questioning"; *What They Bring: The Poetry of Migration and Immigration* (International Psychoanalytic Books, 2020): "Asad's Father Asks What He Remembers," "Kwashiorkor"; *Writing Fire: An Anthology Celebrating the Power of Women's Words* (Green Fire Press, 2017): "London Asks to be Remembered."

Special thanks to Lise Goett, poetry doula extraordinaire, as well as to the poets of the San Miguel Poetry Week and the Crossing Paths group for their critical readings of many of these poems.

Cover photo: RCW 7 ("A transformation in progress"), ESA/Hubble & NASA, J. Tan (Chalmers University & University of Virginia), R. Fedriani (Institute for Astrophysics of Andalusia). Photo of author by Regine Jackson. Book designed and typeset by Judith Kerman in Chaparral Pro with titles in Book Antiqua.

Contents

I
In the Beginning ... 5
The Arsonist Addresses the Gods ... 6
The Fire Responds to Questioning ... 7
After the Dying ... 8
And If It Is Beautiful ... 9
Remix: The Paper Brigade ... 11
Towards the Starting Points ... 12

II
The Universe Considers Loss ... 17
London Asks to Be Remembered ... 19
Visible ... 20
Blind Earl Teacup ... 21
Autumn Letter ... 22
Remix: A Story of This Xmas Eve Before Being Dished Out ... 23
Kwashiorkor ... 25
Of War and Seizure ... 26

III
Sew Me into Your Country ... 29
How To Become a Raft ... 31
8 Separations ... 32
Waiting in Line at Immigration ... 34
Miguel ... 35
Four Postcards ... 36
Marta ... 37
Ten-Day Forecast ... 38
Alejandra ... 39
Ghazal: Home ... 40
Asad's Father Asks What He Remembers ... 41
Remix: In Defense of Kherson ... 43

IV
Galactic Neighborhoods ... 47
Home: a Cadralor ... 48
One of Those Towns Lined with Empty Factories ... 49
The Lost Colony, After Christmas ... 50
Between Damage and Lighthouse ... 51
Frank ... 53

Edmonia Lewis Carves Hagar	54
American	55
Suffer the Little Children	56
Lemon Tree	57

V

Analemma	61
On the Origin of Love	62
Love,	63
The Wandering Albatross	64
You Taught Me	65
Prayer in the New Year	66
Ecce Mundus	68
Oh, My Beloveds	70
Ode to the Universe	72
About the Author	73
Note	73

I

In the Beginning

story > Greek historia = *a learning through inquiry*

I ask the sky
and it tells me it was born
from cloudseed
while the sea rose
from a murmur
into the breath of night.

I ask the fish
and it tells me it has no memory
of a time before being—
a shaft of light
wavered through water
and it fed.

I ask the sun and it says
its birth
was the birth of appetite
and is endless.

I ask war
and it says it regrets
everything
but that all the fear
in the world has to fuel
something.

I ask fear and it recounts
its first dream—
dark whispers around corners
and the carmine scent
of fire.

I ask the trees
and they say they carry flame
like blood
waiting to be ignited.

I ask love
and it opens itself to me
in silence.

The Arsonist Addresses the Gods

Which of you remembers the galaxy
furrowed before my birth, my future
before the past that was yet to arrive—

flames seeking their own consumption—
the books in the library, that story
I never told, not even to myself in darkness?

Such memories cannot be withstood easily—
even by gods. I see you flinch.
You are not spared any more than I,

my heart, its pages blazing in beautiful
annihilation. Which of you
holds the seeds of my disaster

written on the shore, unspooling line
describing the continent, its blue edge
winding into space? Oh,

each heart is broken.
I need a god who can fit our globe
into the acorn I finger in my pocket.

The books burn ever.
I can do no more than to be alive
in the face of memory's undoing.

The Fire Responds to Questioning

Yes, I was there.

No, I did not call for help.

I don't know how I started.

What I remember is warming into being,
first my extremities, fingers of light
flickering, then only a gust of wind
and suddenly I was everywhere,
burning with hunger.

Linen drapes flared yellow
and glowed behind me.
Books smoked. A woolen armchair
sputtered orange while a pair of cranes
on a Chinese silk screen shrank from me.
The cranes smelled like charred meat.
The books blackened.

No, I didn't content myself with the library.
I spread out, made myself at home,
tried each bed, filled each dresser.

Understand, I hardly had time to think.
Someone dreamed me into life
and all I knew was doubling,
every thirty seconds doubling.

Tell me: what do you know
of how you began?
What did you burn as you grew?

After the Dying

Nothing but gray—crosshatched gray
earth, gray sky charred to the horizon
through gray-scale branches. Then comes

rain, cupfuls in drops, and the rivers
reborn, soil learning again
to drink, violets rising to split gray

into green and purple. The ash trees
still stand bleak in their nakedness
but grass grows once more between them.

Soon a deer, who survived the fires
but lost her world to their darkening,
moves in, foraging, mouth open

to receive it—a banquet of color,
its light touch bathing her tongue.

And If It Is Beautiful

If I knew whose fault the fire was
would I delete my memories

of sleepless nights
raging against the spark that started it

and turn my fury
towards the hapless human

whose negligence or curiosity
or malice or lack of understanding

smoldered into flame
then soot

and ashes?
Or would I dream

of blazing immolations—
theirs as imagined penance

and my own
in cremation after death,

our bodies shrinking
and joints flexing

into our last pugilistic pose?
No life was lost in the inferno.

Only spaces shaped
by the lives lived in them—

Helen's jar of wooden spoons,
George's armchair in the library—

lives unknowing who to blame
or if that person might deserve

more sadness than anger,
their own peace

burned through
as they stood watching

flames that must have been
in their own way beautiful.

Remix: The Paper Brigade

> *The horrors of the Holocaust were met with various forms of resistance. [A] resistance group nicknamed the Paper Brigade ... in what is now Vilnius, Lithuania's capital ... risked death, smuggling artwork, books and rare manuscripts - hiding them in underground bunkers.*

Gun, of totalitarianism. Bounty, but of totalitarianism. Evil filled in. So to the ghetto.

The ghetto had other ideas. Dug up the survive out of the brutal looting. Dug up the survive: this culture, these boxes. Materials the ghetto.

Years, it encompassed. This is the absence that could never emerge from hiding. They set aside the scooped-empty heroes, homemade wheelbarrow and shovels. The building organ. The church now tunnel.

Anything in—saved. Anything needed for kindling, baroque arches, wiped out country. Dusty iron knocked down, the rubble a manuscript.

Deliverer upon faded saved. Collection of works rescued and lives of beauty walking. Book Palace an absence that could never rubble. Erasure knocked down, became human of the burnt contraband. Surviving pages insisted books had blood. Vanished Book the war.

The other ideas, floor to the gun, rooms upon rooms. Paper could never, wasn't bounty. Bellows the war, wiped out nexus of poetry, what you're not allowed. You weren't taught books. *No. No.*

Picture those Jews encompassed, amplified by Chagall. Insisting feet down, assessing and prescient. Their hiding places. Their hiding places. Fearing the so says who. Heard whispers. Documents would were killed.

The evil is full, the *it* encompassed. Yiddish voices the unexplored absence that stains. This unexplored Book absence out of the burnt readers, contraband community.

These are the surviving pages. Homemade diapers sewn Nazi, sewn Red Army. The us there, awaiting renovation. Who we have. Who we have: the scooped fragments.

Towards the Starting Points

Language always already displaced as if stolen when, in reality, it was imposed, the conqueror laying stones on the tongues of the subjugated, their weight the burden of violence.

Between one shore and the other, waves crisscrossing, vowels lengthening, shortening.

My ancestors were mostly among those who thought they knew best and yet knew the New World was unknown, unknowable. They lie inside me, in the spirals of my DNA. Even the place names they borrowed twisted almost beyond recognition—Muswachasut, Mishigami.

Language as what we taste when we speak. Language as sustenance. Language as mother. In the lands my forefathers occupied, Mishigami, mother was nimaamaa. In the lands I now inhabit, Muswachasut: my mother—ngok, your mother—kok.

The first tongue I heard, in the clinic where I was born, was oxymoronic—Venezuelan Spanish—far from Spain, its decentered origins betrayed by missing sibilants as the nurses swirled. Vamo a Caraca our family code for the country of my birth, a stubborn absence.

From one perspective, continents awaited. From another, they were the world.

Is a chant the same as a song? Is a star a sentence? Is the ocean the secret dream of night? Once I camped on a volcano, the grasses on its slopes like hair leaning into the thin air of sunset. All night I mouthed its name: Popocatepetl, Popocatepetl.

Those were the days I dwelled in the rising pitches of Mexican Spanish, its many syllables. They rolled in my mouth like pebbles worn smooth from abrasion. At Candelaria, the churches were filled with baby dolls to be blessed, el niño Jesús, many dressed in white to harness the power of the sun god. Huitzilopochtli, Christ, la Virgen, Totec.

American English, too, oxymoronic, and I caught in the middle, rhoticity an American palimpsest bleeding under my British lexicon and high falling intonations. My mother's tongue, my father's tongue, the Atlantic rolling between them.

When ancestry whispers, it speaks in riddles, while the bells on the parish church toll for joy, for sorrow, for gathering. Fireworks explode. The long slow churn of currents circle, one coast to another.

In the Aztec calendar, I was born on the day of Cipactli—god of creation, god of fertility. God of the land, a great earth monster, floating on the sea of stars. The Catholic calendar honors St. Boniface, who cut down the Sacred Oak of Geismar, consecrated to Thor. When the sky is clear, I like to locate the Pleiades, Thor's hammer, Mjölnir—

this too a language of my ancestry, the language of the name I was given when I was born in Venezuela: my mother's mother's mother's name. A heritage of sea captains. In this way, English too spun from borrowings, from impositions, dǫnsk tunga laid on Anglo-Saxon, my heritage a weft of woven threads, a constellation of continents.

My life a moment. My tongues mine, not mine, heavy, weightless, liquid, and made of fire.

II

The Universe Considers Loss

Last night the treetops wiped a piece of sky
clean like a deep blue blackboard

as they flounced in the wind, shaking
their leaves into the air. Dark grey removed,

we could see inside the sky
clear through the atmosphere to where

nothing is, mostly enormous nothing,
punctuated by fires and rocks,

all minute in the scheme of the universe.
In this scale, a stone is a stone

is a stone, casting small ripples of gravity
to hold its surface—or maybe even us—to its core

as it hauls its way toward an ever-receding
edge with whatever lies outside nothingness.

Come, we'll share the heavy lifting
of grasping so much of so little.

As usual, we'll find ourselves capable
of much more than we could have imagined

possible. That's true of many things.
We keep waiting for the rest

of our dead ash tree's limbs to come down
but they refuse to snap, even in winds

like we had last night. The music
the leaves made dancing was the sound

of erasure—first there were clouds
and then none. No, that's not it.

First there were clouds and then
the clouds changed form—not empty,

only invisible. Transparent,
so we could acquire stars.

London Asks to Be Remembered

Remember Aunt Pam, it says,
remember Elsa, remember

even your great-grandmother
you never knew, her shape

shrinking to no more than smoke
as the bombs she hid from in the Underground

continued to echo, refusing her
any peace but death. My mother

had been a child then, dumb
to language that could speak such things—

besides, of war, what is there to say?
Life went on. And later,

when I was a child in London, too,
I held my mother's hand

passing her old flat, walking
the same paths in the same parks.

On Sundays, I behaved my way through dinner
with great-aunts and -uncles,

and, hovering, all the absent ones—
Pam's Timmy...

their father, Frederik, dead young...
their mother, Mama Lisken,

she of the bombs, she for whom
my mother named me.

Visible

Family lore suggested heroism:
Uncle Timmy sacrificed himself to save the lives of his squadron.

I search the web—*RAF Group Captain, missing believed killed, March 1, 1942, Java*—find no evidence one way or the other.

Mostly blind by the time I knew her, my great-aunt Pam endured,
listened to BBC World News on her black transistor radio,

her husband neat in his uniform
framed on the bookshelf behind the tea caddy.

My husband is scrolling news as I research,
shows me pictures of next-generation fighter jets,

their advanced stealth airframes and avionics. *Nearly invisible*, he marvels.
We don't know what kind of bomber Timmy flew.

At 90, Pam moved into a tiny bedsit at a rest-home.
On my final visit, she declined to speak of herself, asked instead

after my work and my husband. I brought freesias
and set them on the windowsill above the clanking, ineffective radiator.

I recognized nothing from her home
but the radio—and Tim on the bedside table.

When I left, she walked me to the top of the stairs
feeling along the wall

and waited there in her slippers until I called up
that I was safely landed at the bottom.

Blind Earl Teacup

> *The 18th century "Blind Earl" china pattern was named after the blind fifth Earl of Coventry. Legend has it that he requested a raised design so that he could feel the pattern.*

Goddammit, she loved that cup,
the feel of its slim handle, its gold rim,

raised vines circling the bowl for the earl
to trace the pattern with his fingers,

eyes clouded by blindness. When she
dropped it, hands clumsied by illness,

closed buds fell in fragments, sharp edges
that were not there the instant before.

Was the earl always blind, or did darkness
arrive gradually? We can't know what's next,

so much coming into being—now, and now,
and in each increment between each now,

tongue pressed behind the teeth to sound the *n*,
mouth rounding for *ow* as it would close

to take a sip of tea—and so much now leaving.
We picked up the fragments,

finished our tea chatting about our childhoods.
Now when I visit her widower: silence

where there was conversation, cold kettle,
saucer without its cup, alone in the cabinet.

Autumn Letter

—to my nursery school fiancé, Benjamin

Sorting was the first life skill
they taught us: light or dark,
square or triangular, real
or imaginary. I got good at it,
took a job organizing shoe boxes
and measuring feet
on metal gauges like sundials,
children standing tall, lengthening
their shadows to claim *Size 12!*

You learned well, too, Benjamin,
as I hear you deal in columns every day—
round numbers, bottom lines, organizational
pyramids—while a son no doubt
has outgrown the old family rocking horse
we rode at your fourth birthday
as the sun set in the bay window
and our shadows galloped across
the pavement. In those days

we believed in God, and certainty,
and lining up in front of the fire
to sing and march in place
just like the Grand Old Duke of York's
ten thousand men, happy
and dutiful. In the park, we stomped
on each other's shadows.
You're probably still Church of England,
barely. But, Benjie, what is the shape
of fading? The hue of absence?
Do you know—when God died,
what happened to his shadow?

Remix: A Story of This Xmas Eve Before Being Dished Out

On Christmas Eve of 1914, five months into World War I, something amazing happened: thousands of British and German troops on the Western Front decided to put down their weapons, rise from the trenches, and greet each other peacefully.

Germans gathered round,
big fires blazing
and we between the lines
calling to one another.

      Until 9 pm when War begins again.

They talked, introduced us properly.
He asked, said "yes."
I was astonished at the easy way.

      Smoke the game.
      Morning the game.

A happy Xmas, he sang.
Fixed up peace in a day,
natural and friendly.

      Tomorrow we shall be men—
      two lines hard at it.
      I am the trench.

All the time safe.
Pork chop. Plum pudding.
Mince pies.
Wine and a cigar.

      Between the lines they bury their dead.

A happy Xmas, he sang.
A fine voice.
Our men calling to another.
Songs and conversation.

      Guns in the distance and the occasional rifle shot.
      Moonlit night, the killing one another.

English and broken English.
Germans only wishing for no shooting.

      Until shooting begins again.
      Tomorrow we shall be bodies
      only wishing for peace.
      Tomorrow we shall be air.

A happy Xmas, he sang,
sang a solo to small lights.
Each side clapped
and sat on the parapet.

      Tomorrow we shall be at it hard again.

All the same, here I am.

I have been within trenches
in peace.

Kwashiorkor

Entire villages meander from hunger to hunger
enticed by small scraps, the scrapings of a bowl
hallucinating meat and banquets on tables
savoring saliva in dreams between wakings
silencing the children with pebbles like sweets

Empty is the normal condition of the bowls
mothers place carefully on shelves behind basins
harvest failed again in sun's conspiracy with rain
bellies distended as if in mockery of my prosperity
each child weaned another body ballooning

Of the dreams of the fathers away working
I can say nothing except that they are also empty
cries of their children silent across the miles
open mouths turned upward like baby birds'
hunger eating the fathers too yes hunger

Of War and Seizure

ruin from bombs   smoke-shrouded   in aerial images

    as if slaughter   happened only   at a distance

pooled blood   blotting an MRI   of my sister's brain

how we are seized   damage overflowing

    you   being also I   and both of us   no   one

but one   with all the others

    targets circled   *old blood*

    not knowing   what might   befall

      each of us   at any moment

       coup-contrecoup

      strike or   retaliation

        drone victim   or surgical subject

strategic arteries   clouded   behind the blurring

    subdural hematoma   and   subterranean concussion

I am ashamed   to find the maps   beautiful

    brain magnetically realigned

      contours   of land   traced by satellites

      my sister

        all the sisters

III

Sew Me into Your Country

Carry me—
a shape formed of water and bone,

a creature transferred from potentiality
to body—

across your threshold—
Sweep me

beyond the looping river—
a form stitched through—

needle up,
needle down—

as destiny
lifted into an upswept mountain—

Weave me
into your fabric—

gather my threads
into the weft of your land.

Lead me across the mountain
as by decree—

beyond frontiers,
political or geographical—

their conditional condition—
to transcend creation,

or the limits of it—
to transpose the accidents,

transcribe the loss,
turn it to substance—

as birth—
or lovers

who pass the night
flung across each other—

arms forming crosses.

How To Become a Raft

The waves remember only wind,
but you've seen water lapping onto shore,
thinning into nothing.

When you meet petrels, watch
how they rise from the ocean into the sky
and float there, their horizon land.

Climb to the tops of the waves.

You'll see jellyfish,
all the kinds that ever scared you—
lion's manes,
blooms of medusas.

Lash yourself to the air with their loose tentacles.
They've been detached a long time
and no longer sting.

Remember when you were nine—
a moon-white beach,
dark water glittering.

Coat yourself in phosphorescence.

Remember, you wanted to be the ocean,
to gleam like that.

8 Separations

1

Dark grids cast by grillwork
onto orange dirt
grow tighter and tighter
as the sun rises into the sky.
Two steel serpents stretch
across desert and mountains,
stare through red camera eyes.

2

Concrete wall segments, watch-towers, anti-tank ditches, minefields.
No one in sight.
Dry silence.

3

A column of men pushes bales of clothing
along a red-dusted path
next to steel fence and razor wire.
Women bent at forty-five degrees press
through blue turnstiles, backs stacked
with shoes, drinks, blankets roped
to their shoulders, secured with duct tape.

4
A weakened ocelot trots alongside.

5

A man in military uniform on a platform
peers through a high-power telescope
from behind bullet-proofed glass.

6

For 120 miles, a striped blanket on the landscape—

berm
    ditch
        chain-link fence
            razor wire
                electrified wire
                    second berm
                        second ditch
                            empty swath
                                iron wall
                                    asphalt road.

Helicopters hover.

7

A concrete barrier
in vertical segments carves
an irregular and continuous S
contoured to the houses on the hillsides
as if shrink-wrapping the neighborhoods.

Uprooted olive trees lie dying in a bulldozed strip of restricted land.

8

The longest yet—almost 900 miles and growing,
double row of electrified fencing filled with concertina wire,
networked by thermal imagers, light systems, alarms.
Here and there, a crater
where a mine
exploded

someone.

Waiting in Line at Immigration

There is plenty of time to consider
your geography—no longer wherever on earth

you flew in from, but not yet officially
anywhere else, your bag at your feet,

weight alternating from left leg to right.
One family several lanes over has been

fingerprinted and photographed,
has been standing at their kiosk forever.

The mother has one child on her hip,
another squirming under her hand on his head.

A chime rings when another lane opens
to relieve the pressure, like a new sluice

for disgorging people onto the land. Two guards
at the front of the cordoned switchbacks

control the faucets. When in the end your passport
is stamped and you are welcomed home

without difficulty, you must reclaim
your map, ink coordinates back in.

Now you are here. X marks the spot.
This land is your land. They said so.

Miguel

I.

You asked me why I didn't look back:
I was afraid to. What if God punished me
like Lot, turned me into a pillar or a tree?
Or turned you into a tree and me
into a bird without flight feathers,
blown along the ground away from you,
never rising high enough to see
a horizon on whose other side
I can at least imagine you.

II.

Think of me when you turn out the light.

III.

You can't believe how cold it is here.
My breath is ice-locked, cuts me from inside.
I wrap myself in all the clothes I have,
but I am glass, ready to shatter.

IV.

Do you still sing every morning
while you are dressing? When I think of you
I hear melody like honey or light
streaming through stained glass
like the Sun Man in Toluca—
golden fire, bright song reaching.

V.

At night I try to remember us together.
But all the space between us
comes down to one line,
drawn west to east as if
with thick black marker.

VI.

Pray for us.

Four Postcards

3 May

It's hard to find postcards at all here
so the picture on the front
looks nothing like what I wanted
to show you—this morning,
for instance, me, sitting on a park bench
with sun in my eyes and pigeons
at my feet, writing to you.

10 May

I've marked my neighborhood
with an X—top right, see?
It's a long walk from there
to here, where they take pictures
and sell postcards. I'll carry
the taste of the stamp back with me,
on my tongue, through the winding streets,
as the perfect bird wings its way to you.

17 May

Add dogs barking. Add car horns.
Add a train bleating its inevitable way
through the night, through the long valley.
Add waking up thinking that your head
is where your feet are. Add waking up
thinking that your heart is where
someone else is. Take away the sunrise,
the brightness blessing the scene.

24 May

I wonder, have you been receiving my cards?
Do they come evenly spaced, as I send them,
every Monday? Or do they clump together,
grimy and mangled? I write neatly, but
the woman at the post office handles them
roughly. I think that she does not believe
in you. I wonder, do you believe in me?

Marta

For four years, a shadow
        has covered her, cross-hatched

and looming: tight grid
        of metal barrier rising

to sky. On Sunday
        she will approach it. On each side

a row of people will raise their arms.
        A guitarist will begin playing

and voices will mingle in stereo
        and compete with the whine

of a passing Border Patrol ATV.
        Two small altars will hold

almost identical chalices, and priests
        on either side will break bread

at the same moment. When the service
        is over, Marta will touch

her daughter's finger, still small enough
        to reach through layers of grille.

She will shake her head at her husband—no,
        no word on status. No change.

Small wooden crosses lean against the fence,
        words painted in green, purple, red—

No olvidamos.
        We don't forget.

Ten-Day Forecast

1   Today's origin is thunder.
        Expect turbulence.

2   The windsocks have changed direction.
        Shh. Let me whisper my lies to you.
        It will be alright. Everything will be alright.

3   A river is growing.
        A city is up to its neck
        and the river keeps growing.

4   The night watch patrols in cloaks.
        Whatever goes dark in your heart
        blots out a star. We are equal parts
        radiance and ink.

5   Shining, shining, blinding.
        Sun, water. Water, water.
        Black indelible water.

6   No one can advise the weather vane.
        In the coal of night
        it trembles unseen.

7   Those at sea will scan
        for the unexpected.
        On land, wind
        will make mazes in cornfields.

8   Back to your heart and its darkness:
        your blood strokes as the storm
        tracks, your voice near-naked.

9   Oars are lifted as in salute,
        saints appealed to. Wind's tenor
        a continuo, an oscillation.

10   Only debris and condensation
        make tornados visible.
        I have tried to foretell your future
        for the last time.

Alejandra

This home is not bougainvillea climbing
high walls topped by blue sky impossible,
is not dust blooming in my nostrils,
not stone and slate and cold polished tile.
This home doesn't ring like morning birdsong,
doesn't smell like sugar and lemonade,
overlooks no saints, no mariachi parade.
This home creaks woodenly all night long.
No bees would dance directions to this home.
Its door looms gold in no one's nightly dream,
goes walking nowhere, is only what it seems.
This home is skeleton, is rib and ice-bone.
I beat drums, burn incense, herb every wall.
Still I'm a stranger, with no home at all.

Ghazal: Home

Do you tell guests to "make themselves at home"?
I always freeze at that: what do I do to make myself at home?

We moved so often when I was growing up it seems a miracle
my mother unpacked every box each time to set us up with home.

There's lots of houses no guest ever goes in,
until an ambulance is summoned, an emergency at home.

When Covid brought on lockdowns no one went anywhere.
I counted how few cars per minute passed by my home.

At five, I was full English. At nine, American. At summer camp,
I crossed my fingers behind my back pledging to a flag as home.

I look around my room: art, knickknacks, books, worn furniture.
How would a stranger judge me, judging from this home?

Most days I find the phone exhausting.
I confess at times I've asked my husband to say I'm not at home.

"Where are you from?" is an easy question for my husband.
I have to pick an age, a year, before I can name a home.

In that most American of pastimes, baseball, everything depends
upon leaving—and then returning to—home.

Floods, bombings, earthquakes, inability to work—
across the world 150 million people have no home.

England taught me to hear class, America to see it.
Either way, Lisken, unpack. Make yourself home.

Asad's Father Asks What He Remembers

Scarf tied under my chin,
we walked through cemeteries,
through muddy fords, through
cratered streets, through woods.

Once, someone was playing
a violin: I could see the notes
cascading from a high window,
their yellows, blues, reds

almost too much to bear,
but pretty—not like the shelling
that drowned me in oceans
of clashing color. Had I known then

that you didn't see sound, would I
have told you, Father? I don't know.
I bent and folded wild grasses
in my fingers as we walked,

sucked on pebbles.
When the bats appeared, swiping
across our path, rest was coming.
Sometimes even a pillow.

More often not. Cities
had subways, which felt safe
but when the buskers began,
the colors bounced off walls

and were blinding. At home,
there had been a lion in the zoo.
When I saw a toy one in a store window,
I said nothing, and we walked on.

I saw women and wondered
if anyone ever got a new mother.
I did have her cardigan,
slept with it at night.

That, and a stone from her grave.
I know now the one thing you took
was a photo of her.
Why didn't you show it to me?

At every border,
the guards were in dark green,
like thunder. From before,
I remember only the lion.

Remix: In Defense of Kherson

How Citizen Spies Foiled Putin's Grand Plan for One Ukrainian City: A partisan cell in Kherson spied on, undermined and even hunted down Russian soldiers.

1

Insurgent shush in their small kitchen, some old hunting rifles, arguing over whom. Under the Russians' noses, what was possible suffered so much. Life was getting grim. Resistance changed tactics. It went underground. An assembly of ordinary people, an inflatable dinghy, a glimmer of hope.

2

Guns, fear and paranoia didn't give far to first days—something about local fighters on imperial rifles. Aging Ukrainian fishermen on a foggy beach ratcheted up the pressure to ambush a Russian column. Money and violence concealed years ago banded together to repel the crisp camouflage forces of Mr. Putin's Soviet army. Still their country.

3

Days after the invasion, the black grenades. Tried cutting through will. Cutting through map coordinates. They used code. Location, a password to circulate. Concealed guns. Ukrainians who themselves had war families killed enemy soldiers. Everything Russian military symbol. The frozen ground a strategic funnel.

4

Grenades a rash, disturbing in the dark while countless people just kept finding avenues. A terrified direction of travel. No small risk. Russian patrols prowling, electric shocks and sadistic beatings. Few weapons, the mist. Propaganda billboards. But the residents knew. Hovering over each other—students, mechanics, grandmothers. They of resistance. They a population of about 300,000 local work.

5

The glass of vodka before every never. They became steeled to emerging. By the waterfront, pretending. Hardware stores of yellow ribbons mysteriously appeared. Their city, buying yellow paint. Buying yellow travel. A glow settled over warm bodies, shipbuilding plants servicing flame on the stove. Russian woolen hats had begun to flee.

6

Veteran fishermen stood in their square joining the crowds of owners, celebrating the city's liberation. They who had filtered messages quietly kissed a policeman, their faces ruddy. Thank everyone, everyone. Every defiance. Resistance a blue river, rushing home.

IV

Galactic Neighborhoods

Cosmological walls

    separate

        one cluster from another—

            our home galaxy

                a flat arrangement of vast islands

                stars and dust

            velocities

                surrounded by voids—

similar

    relative to expansion

        but a billion light years across—

                disruptive pasts

        nothing

                out of the ordinary—

    our dark matter

        a strong influence

                assuming some peculiar lack—

yet halos

        extend

                beyond the visible

Home: a Cadralor

1

What to call the color of heat
simmering above sand and ocean?
The elongated horizon pulses beyond.
Focus dissolves into the spectrum.
I remember the sharp cool clarity of night.

2

When I was a child I helped my father stack logs
near the house, gusts almost knocking me
to my knees. Then we shut ourselves in
and I watched from the window the pitiless
wind pummel the shore, hostility absent.

3

The air in this canyon is a voice
echoing in a cathedral. We vibrate
in sympathy and rise to exist in it.
At sunset, amber and firebrick
set against our faces.

4

Define yourself, says my dream, and the glass
I am holding falls without breaking, caught
by a soft shawl that moments ago was wrapped
around me. I wake to find it is snowing,
huge flakes filling the air, like a ceiling dissolving.

5

The whole world spun when I flicked
my grandpa's globe, suspended in the nest
of its stand, stopped where my finger landed—
Jaipur, Shanghai, an empty stretch of the Atlantic.
And then I'd measure how many hands to home.

One of Those Towns Lined with Empty Factories

Towns where once the factories defined what it was to be human
factories processing widgets and time cards punched by pale humans
humans and machines whirring and clicking like windmills
metal winding machines like windmills—

I knew a human who was wound by a winding machine
when the safety platform failed
her body banded by the scars she lived with afterwards
her matchstick frame compacted—

In places along the river there are gaps
where there used to be factories
now there is nothing but if you follow the river
you'll reach a quarry—

Once they carved marble out of the quarry
they pulled slabs and dimension stone out of the quarry
the marble was the quarry
the money from the marble was the quarry—

Now the quarry is filled with water
the water filling the quarry is unbearably cold
the marble must be unbearably cold underwater
the marble once cut for tombs lies underwater—

I knew a human who dove weighted into the hole
it was so clear and so beautiful
so beautiful and cold and the marble blocks so sharp
at the bottom of the quarry and what was he supposed to do—

there were no jobs at the factories any longer
what was a human to do
no jobs cutting marble any longer no money
this human so beautiful and now nothing

The Lost Colony, After Christmas

Now that it's time to dismantle the tree,
pillage its branches for ornaments
to re-wrap, re-box, re-stow,
like root cellar provisions for the next
dark season—
                now that it's time,
I don't want to.

        Our era an era
of restless dark hemmed in by flags,
pikes, lies rusted into place, crosses
brandished or fired, fear—
                    what harm
if our straw angel perches a little longer
in the cactus dish, our tree's lit bulbs
reflected in the window behind it?

We take our light where we can.

How long did the settlers have
before they took down their palisades,
carved messages in trees, vanished?

How far across
those broad sounds and estuaries

        could a small fire be seen?

Between Damage and Lighthouse

It isn't easy, she says, this living,
how it hurts

constantly, the beauty
and the unthinkable,

the faith in my child's face
and the fact of children drowning,

the fox sliding across the lawn
and the night ahead of her

alive and killing. On every scale,
she says, it isn't easy—

my ash trees dying, eaten
from the inside out, my heart

struggling against containment, against
its countdown hammering

my ribs. We want
and don't want. I know

a boy, she says, who gouged *hate*
into his arm after his mother

hanged herself for him to find her.
Grown now, he's inked it over.

Still life isn't easy for him,
like when his dog who was the center

of his ground got cancer—
what was he to do with that—

but he insists on loving, all while
his heart and the world batter him.

So much hangs in the balance
between damage and lighthouse,

between words carved into your own skin
and words transparent.

Do you understand, she says.
This living's precarious.

Frank

Frank cradles his rifle
as if it poured sanctified water
from its maw instead of bullets.
This is how he mourns his mother.

She died last year at home in Dayton,
a box of Kleenex by her head and no
phone calls though she checked hourly.
He waits for the light of dawn,

half-dreams of ice cream and the tigers
he used to visit at the zoo, the moat
between them. He'd stare and stare
but they never looked back.

He has no mirror, gave it away
the first time he shot a man,
wanting nothing to do with faces
anymore. He tries to get his tongue

around the names of places—
Al-Qa'im, Jalalabad—tries to imagine
growing up wrapped in these sounds.
When he was a boy

he read stories about war—
a cave, a frightened horse running.
He wishes he had a horse.
It could carry him through the long nights.

He used to read with a flashlight
under the covers until his mother
took the book from him. He wishes
his mother had been a horse.

Edmonia Lewis Carves Hagar

If in the course of chiseling
I gouge her eye, shatter her nose—
what do I do?

Hagar knows about survival
as well as I—
         stony silence,
     injustice of expulsion
     for sins that were not ours.

Metamorphic rock like this
understands resistance, too,
inhabits hardness— its own
and the battering—

     in the beginning
     it was pearls and snails
     ground to slow limestone,
     crystallized only
     under pressure, heat
     birthing marble.

Hagar founded
a race of kings.

I rasp her hair back,
tilt her chin up,
     chisel anew.

American

There's a secret in my throat behind a locked door and no key
but only ragged edges marking the trajectory of its entry rasping
and ants that scurry in circles as if to protect something
and nothing I can do to soften or dislodge it.

I swallow past the secret, raw like a wound, red like a wound gaping—
but don't go thinking I need your sympathy, this isn't a cry for help
or some kind of confession, this is simply a statement of fact
and the fact is we all have the same wound, our country gasping.

I can't name the secret to disarm it—even whatever residue
the ants find is gone before I see it and nothing to give me clues
but the wall, the lock, and the blood coming at me
and the blood coming at all of us, even the children

and all we do is stare at each other. I try to speak to you
but my mouth has become a muzzle and my voice
a bullet scored by rifling and spun into flight. Here—
I will open wide and we can look down the barrel together.

Suffer the Little Children

even the clouds have settled in as if stasis has become
the only proper mode now that children are dead
how can we process that except by standing still
at this edge suddenly visible and steep
it's crazy to keep going

but a cold wind blowing across the cliff
presses into us demands our attention
the clods of earth we kicked loose carelessly
careen over the precipice along with everything
we had imagined and now almost visualize

small faces laughing and crying
our own that are no longer small and others
we don't recognize all blur into fog
what was moving now perpetually motionless
we don't say anything

only place our palms together and bow
and begin to walk leaning against the wind
grass ground to dirt beneath our feet
the cliff a wall and at its base plastic toys
wrapped presents hats coats school photos

the wind has blown something out of us
what is the sense we have been left with
as we walk on in the endless face of falling
the only sound the absence of voices
our hands closing on air and we the precipice

Lemon Tree

another child has been shot
                        a classmate is standing on a podium
    last week it snowed for three days
                            today I see crocuses
next week I am leaving on vacation to Mexico
                millions have never left on vacation
      today another child has drowned
                       yesterday I fell asleep to the sound of rain
  a section of the Pacific is nothing but plastic
              in Ukraine children drink radioactive milk
our coral reefs are bleaching repeatedly
              in Yemen there is nothing to drink
    tomorrow will be another work day
        tonight will be another work night for those who work nights
  I know the ease that it is to have a good life
                I wonder what it means to live a good life
in Fukushima cars in lanes are swallowed by vines
                          Pripyat is still a ghost city
    another child has died
                  hundreds demonstrate at Park Square
this snow flurry will not amount to anything
      in my life I live among the dead
    in my dreams I visit with the living
              our lemon tree is finally putting out new leaves

v

Analemma

Today the sun
is a victory—victoriously re-
turning to the same place

> it was a year ago, heirloom
> from the earth's past—air
> weaving the fine flax

>> of light arced by our curvature,
>> vatic messages from our star—
>> tomorrow we will be here

> and then here and where-
> ever the sun spins us
> as it shrinks into itself—

I have marked its position
each day, elliptic
and tilt, ecliptic and—

> wait, I am leaving out
> night, I am circum-
> locuting the location of the moon—

>> let me not omit the moon—
>> its return thirteenfold over the sun—
>> with us at its center—

> sunlit and moonlit, our planet's
> species woven in constellations,
> waxing and waning—

and I too fusing and cycling, re-
fusing to leave the orbit
of my life, each day a victory.

On the Origin of Love

Or a single bat hawked across the sky
and lighted in the sconce of your chest.

Or you watched as the sun crested the mountain
and the town caught fire
to begin the day.

Or my dream conjured you
and you became an owl, blending invisibly
with the bark behind you,
your eyes two knots in the trunk.

Or you dreamed me.

Or it was my fault
and you were hypnotized—
or vice versa.

Or nothing happened at all
and we are still dreaming.

Or you heard the bat before you saw it,
its chittering the sound of a heart waking.

Or a heart floundering.

Or when the owl flew over the town
nothing else moved
except flames.

Or the deepening dark of nightfall
consumed you
and when you reached to feel your way
there I was.

Love,

tell me about the time
we fell in love

and didn't know it,
arguing about us and *argue* versus *discuss*,

your black Thunderbird purring beneath us
in the parking lot of your inconsolable

apartment, the one with the broken steps
and the kitchen table jammed

against the wall and no light anywhere.
How it was almost the end,

me refusing to acknowledge that I could ever *need*
anyone and you

taking that as rejection.
It's not a story like music, more like

the sky had to go somewhere
and that night we went with it.

When we got out of your car,
there was mine, waiting for me to leave.

Tell me how you watched me go
to open the door and how I stopped,

and we walked silently up those broken stairs
and when we reached the top

we kissed, mouths like mirrors.
Tell me again how this is love,

how we never fully understand anyone
but have to try,

taking our chances, even in the dark,
step by tongue by word.

The Wandering Albatross

has the largest wingspan on the planet.
But that's not the question for today—
rather, we must ask who has clothes to wash,
who speaks Papantla Totonac (*moribund*—
i.e., if you do speak it, you are no longer a child),
what to do with your shoes if you have to swim
to get to safety, where to leave the basket
for those who follow and how to carry
what you must take with you.

While you and I were driving the sunlit
sculpted shoreline watching divers
spyhopping like orcas, someone else
was slipping under waves in exhaustion
and not surfacing. Compassion
is not enough, but sometimes it is all
we have to offer. Yearning is the same
for everyone. The albatross spends almost all
its life on the wing, but comes to land for love.

You Taught Me

        that violence is inevitable
though the hawk has waited without success
perched on its branch
for more than an hour as we watched
through the kitchen window
its rust-mottled breast, yellow beak,
its sure conviction—

        and love inevitable too,
how we are drawn together
when apart, sky and earth curving
and flexing like iron filings
between the magnets of our desire—

        and when together,
sex not entirely unlike the swoop
of the hawk, the grip and the claw—

        and that when it is real,
love is all there is—
body-love, hate-love, soul-love—
branches still bare from winter
and the whole world visible,
on guard for ravishing.

Prayer in the New Year

I am nothing if not happy, grateful to be—
which is itself a statement of prayer, here

in this garden that is the world,
the beautiful and the ugly—

bliss in shadows and danger in broad daylight,
the perpetual challenge to propel yourself

from what you know
to what you must do—this too

another way to say what prayer is—reaching
for what is right and true. Though truth

is unsayable, lips and hands meeting
find a grammar that suits them, verbs melting

into nouns, the is-ness of a kiss.
In my dreams I hear words that no longer exist

upon waking, spend my days trying
to write them down. This striving, too—prayer.

Except I pray, how can I live with this stunning—
the bees nosing at the roses, the girls and boys I teach

torn to the core by fear and incredulity, this sky—
again this sky, open without end.

I walk in the valley of the shadow of death
and of life and of life and of life— look at this blade

of grass—I have stepped on it and it has not broken—
and find altars wherever I go—stone wall, desk—

the human, too—breastbone, the dip of a shoulder—
that is, I find places to speak thanks, to you and you and you.

We can choose to hear as little or as much as we wish.
Thus much, today, is asked of you; thus much, tomorrow.

I am called on at least to witness, and to that
I will kneel, I will press my hands together,

I will bow my head to the floor, I will clap
twice—to honor the spirits of the dead and of the living.

Ecce Mundus

I can imagine
based on what I know—

can describe mountains
beyond drawn blinds—

but can say nothing
of guns trained on others.

So much of the world
is black ice

and lacking mercy.

Whatever my intention was,
I leaned and now
I am inside.

As are you,
tilting your ear to my words,
asking me to say what I know.

We want to be in love.
We want to be hooked by love.

This is permitted, concedes the bullet.
You will fall regardless, counters the ice.

    * * *

I mean to be clear—

the mountains we each know
are not the same.

Imagining
slides into dark—

even with the owl standing guard all night
in the tree outside the window,
my dreams will have their victims.

It would be midnight
anytime we let it, you know—

that's how close to the surface
the bullet flies.

* * *

What does the bullet dream?
What do you?

Take my hand—
we will fall together,
day lighting our bones equally.

Here is the owl
rising above the ice
into the black sky.

Here is invisibility,
the ones I cannot see
even in dreams.

I come back to the mountains.
I come back to love.

Still I can conjure nothing
to save them.

Light salts the mountains
and the vulture
takes over for the owl.

Oh, My Beloveds

after Tedi Mills López

what shall I call this
time of moon
time of snowmelt
time of moles
their mounds like small volcanoes
time too of earthquakes
the dispossessed
so many dispossessed
under the same moon
new moon
oh so same old moon
time of tides
and tidal waves
time of drowning
time of desperate
earth downing
what shall I say to this time
blue time
balancing-on-a-knife time
when the dead
do not whisper
how is it that I hear them anyway
dead time
living time
so many buried
under the rubble of the impossible
under glimpses
of mist
open as fields
time of perpetual dusk
time of swallowing dust
time of dust
how should I explain it
to itself
to the dead to my
dead
to the living
to the living dying

while peoples vanish
while glaciers vanish
while waters rise
what tide
can carry these times
oh my beloveds
beyond the apocalypse
our boats leaving
our boats leaking
our lives sinking
in this time
is it ours?

Ode to the Universe

Because, why not? oh most
opalescent everything, mine
of every known mineral,
every unknown element, every
imaginable *oh*, and then some.

Because you're the only modest
proof we have of, well, almost
anything. Maybe not so modest—
enormity inviolate, embodied,
a giantess, beyond our mortal scope.

Because you birth horizons, mermaids,
muddy brooks, black holes.
Because of silver, magnets, homes.

Because I've loved in you, whole lifetimes,
moved by the smell of hazelnut
or dough rising, roused by a lifting
murmur—*do, re, mi*—as I were
tuning fork, song in motion.

Because you let the moon foreshadow us—
our growth, our fall, our need for orbit.
Because you hold us, hold us, every molecule.

About the Author

Lisken Van Pelt Dus is the author of another collection of poems, *What We're Made Of*, as well as two chapbooks, *Everywhere at Once* and *Letters to My Dead*. She was raised in England, the US, and Mexico, and now lives with her husband in western Massachusetts, where she is an award-winning teacher of writing, languages, and martial arts. Her work can be found in many journals, anthologies, and craft books, and has earned several awards and Pushcart Prize nominations.

Note:

The three Remix poems are made of found language, manipulated in part with the help of the Text Mixing Desk of Paul Watson's The Lazarus Corporation. Source texts can be found at the following links:

Remix: The Paper Brigade--*https://www.cbsnews.com/news/paper-brigade-jewish-artifacts-holocaust-60-minutes-2022-11-13/*

Remix: A Story of This Xmas Eve Before Being Dished Out--*https://lettersofnote.com/2015/10/19/the-most-extraordinary-scenes/*

Remix: In Defense of Kherson--*https://www.nytimes.com/2022/12/25/world/europe/ukraine-kherson-defiance-russia.html*

Recent Titles from Mayapple Press...

David Michael Nixon, *A Wolf Comes to My Window*, 2024
        Paper, 40pp, $18.95
        ISBN: 978-1-952781-22-3

Zilka Joseph, *Sweet Melida*, 2024
        Paper, 60pp, $19.95
        ISBN: 978-1-952781-19-3

Eleanor Lerman, *Slim Blue Universe*, 2024
        Paper, 68pp, $20.95
        ISBN: 978-1-982781-17-9

Cati Porter, *Small Mammals*, 2023
        Paper, 78pp, $19.94 plus s&h
        ISBN 978-1-952781-15-5

Eleanor Lerman, *The Game Cafe,* 2022
        Paper, 160pp, $22.95 plus s&h
        ISBN 978-1-952781-13-1

Goria Nixon-John, *The Dark Safekeeping*, 2022
        Paper, 92pp, $19.85 plus s&h
        ISBN: 978-1-952781-11-7

Nancy Takacs, *Dearest Water*, 2022
        Paper, 84pp, $19.95 plus s&h
        ISBN: 978-1-952781-09-4

Zilka Joseph, *In Our Beautiful Bones*, 2021
        Paper, 108pp, $19.95 plus s&h
        ISBN: 9780-1-952781-07-0

Ricardo Jesús Mejías Hernández, tr. Don Cellini,
Libro de Percances/Book of Mishaps, 2021
        Paper, 56pp, $18.95 plus s&h
        ISBN: 978-952781-05-6

Eleanor Lerman, *Watkins Glen*, 2021
        Paper, 218pp, $22.95 plus s&h
        ISBN: 978-1-952781-01-8

Betsy Johnson, *when animals are animals*, 2021
        Paper, 58pp, $17.95 plus s&h
        ISBN: 978-1-952781-02-5

For a complete catalog of Mayapple Press publications, please visit our website at *mayapplepress.com*. Books can be ordered direct from our website with secure on-line payment using PayPal, or by mail (check or money order). Or order through your local bookseller.